WOMAN JOURNEYING

In loving memory of my sister Ann
(Sister Soubirous, I.B.V.M.),
whose wise counsel I sorely miss,
and to John, for his forbearance.

Betty Maher

Woman Journeying

TWO-MINUTE REFLECTIONS ON THE ORDINARY AND THE EVERYDAY

First edition 1994 published by
the columba press
93 The Rise, Mount Merrion, Blackrock, Co Dublin

Cover by Bill Bolger
Origination by The Columba Press
Printed in Ireland by
Genprint Ltd, Dublin

ISBN 1 85607 095 6

The quotation from *Autumn Report* on page 27 is reprinted by permission of Bloodaxe Books Ltd from *Hail! Madam Jazz: New & Selected Poems by Micheal O'Siadhail* (Bloodaxe Books, 1992).

Contents

What shouts of joy, what singing!
Psalm 65

Author's Note

There is also laughter, merriment and
a lightness of touch when God is present.
—Gerard W Hughes, *God of Surprises*

D'accord. And thank goodness none of us travels alone. Others are implicated, and I am deeply indebted to many, some still living, some now gone on ahead, who lightened my way. Certain of these I wish to name:

My parents and those other members of the household in which I grew up and where I first learned the value of diversity in community; my principal teachers of the last thirty years, Ruth, John, Billy, Clare and Barry, who continue to cause me to wonder, to ponder, and therefore to grow; Feena, whose support is beyond measure; Joan, provider of sanctuary, and educator in the truest sense of 'one who draws out'; and Joe, whose unique combination of exasperated patience and fiercely insistent challenging has played its part in causing me to recognise the need to undertake this journey in the first place – no small thing this, but rather it counts for much.

The influence of all of these and others has been, and continues to be of critical importance to me, and not least because, by their loving exactitude in the matter of truth, they have kept me in check – and have lit up my life.

And I am both immensely grateful and profoundly glad.

Betty Maher
October 15, 1993
The feast of St Theresa of Avila

Foreword

Second journeys are often spoken of today and recognised for what they are, an opening up to new inner life in the light of one's earlier experiences. I sense that I was fortunate in that in many respects the commencement of my own second journey coincided with an invitation to contribute some 'Two-minute talks' on radio and television and this invitation, which came out of the blue, gave me the opportunity to collect some of the thoughts and half-thoughts which had been running round my head, and to put some shape on them. Committing them to paper and speaking them on air meant drawing the various strands together in such a way that they might with any luck be understood by others – a salutary task! There is nothing like having to get a point across in minimum time for wonderfully concentrating the mind!

It was then suggested to me that I put these random pieces together in book form and this is the result. I am grateful to those who pressed me to do this, because again it forced me to consolidate. In fact most of the pieces have been reworked, some have merged with others and there are some new pieces which occurred to me as I set about the task. The re-writing seemed necessary because the spoken word does not always happily translate into the written.

As I went about deciding which scripts might be included and which left out, I came to see a movement, a journeying, over the last decade or so. Tentative ideas and half-truths hitherto barely in my consciousness firmed up and as I became aware of this I also realised that this particular journey was clearly and uniquely my own. This is not to say that many others, both women and men, might not have had those same experiences and thoughts but, surrounded – like, I believe, most women of my age – as I have been all my life by a patriarchial world, it was something of a revelation to me to find that my journey had an authenticity of its own; perhaps today younger people will wonder at this – I hope so! The acknowledgement that my journey had its own integrity was an experience of great freedom for me, and in assembling these reflections I would hope that others may find encouragement to seek their own truth out of which to live as they also make their journey.

Finally, I believe that journeys generally have different stages; they have a starting point; then an experiencing; often a recounting, and in the recounting a clearer understanding; and then with that understanding the possibility of moving forward again. That sounds right and it sounds tidy. To put this into practice with these short pieces was less easy, so for help I turned to others' writings, in order to try to bring a semblance of form into the whole. It may help, but has not resulted in complete order. However, perhaps this very randomness is an acknowledgement of the less than tidy reality of most human journeys, and if this small collection has any value then maybe it is in this very fact.

PART I

Journeying

The setting out

Each day the first day: each day a life.

Each morning we must hold out the chalice of our being to receive, to carry, and give back. It must be held out empty – for the past must only be reflected in its polish, its shape, its capacity.

Dag Hammarskjold, Markings

Limitations

I have heard it said by the sages that we are what we are in great part because of our past, and our past is something we cannot change. This means that we are not, as it were, starting from scratch when we set out on our life's journey, but we have been given certain materials, certain limitations, and it is within those limitations and with those materials that we must work.

In other words, we are not creators, but artists. Just as a sculptor has the restrictions of a particular piece of marble, the woodcarver a certain block of wood, an artist the size of his canvas, so too we have been given the basic materials with which to shape ourselves into what we may be.

There is great freedom, I believe, in accepting these limitations. We are born into specific circumstances, in specific places, into specific families, at specific times, and that means that certain things are open to us, and certain things are not. Recognising this simple truth may well, I think, be the real secret of living life to the full. And I am sure that we none of us is asked to do more.

Words

I love words. And I love listening to someone who uses them deftly and accurately. Years ago, I remember reading an essay by William Hazlett in which he said 'I am never less alone than when alone'. I could fully identify with what he was saying. And I also read somewhere that 'We are compelled to go to what we love'. How true and how clear that statement is!

Seamus Heaney once said 'Description is revelation'. And revelation, as we know, is the revealing or exposing of something.

God revealed God's self to us in Christ Jesus, and that man Jesus, was someone who existed totally for others and who came to serve humankind. From what we read of his life, in his presence many were at peace to be considered his friends. One thing they could be sure of was his total integrity.

He also used words with absolute accuracy. And it is worth recalling, I think, that this man said 'Behold, I am with you always, even to the end of time'. To remember this can give courage on the journey.

Small Beginnings

If you look at the source of a river, it's hard to believe that this same trickle of water will eventually become something of great power, irrigating countries, supplying thousands of households with its invaluable resource and eventually adding its drop to the ocean, where it can be used as part of the means of travel from one end of the earth to the other.

And all from such a small beginning. A small beginning, it seems, is the only way. Once, I read a novel where, in the course of a conversation between two people one, trying to make light of a meeting with a third party, said 'It was only a small conversation', and the other replied 'How else does anything begin?' How else, indeed?

We don't need to feel that we must take on the whole world in one fell swoop. We don't need to try to be a river in full spate, carrying great loads across the world. All we need is a small beginning, to learn 'the art of the small'. This may mean taking one small step towards, for instance, healing a relationship, or a small step towards forgiving. We only need to be the source; the rest will follow.

Hospitality

When we invite someone into our homes, we invite that person to see us as we really are, at our heart's core. There's surely truth in the saying 'If you want to know me, come and live with me.'

At the beginning of St John's gospel, some of those who were with John the Baptist were curious about this other man whom John referred to as 'The Lamb of God'. In order to try to know more about him they asked this man where he lived. And he replied 'Come and see'.

We are then told in the story that they did just that, and went with him to his home. And whatever they saw they must have liked, because, the story continues, 'They stayed with him for the rest of the day.'

In fact, we now know that they stayed longer; they stayed with him for life. Jesus, by opening himself and his home to them, made such an impression on them that they gave up their previous lifestyles in order to be with him. And these men for the most part were not youngsters, but men with responsibilities. None the less, they felt called to another way of life with him. It must have taken some explaining to their spouses!

When Jesus said to those men 'Come and see', he said it to us all. The great thing, I suppose, would be if we in return could completely open our hearts to him, and invite him to where we are at our most authentic. It's a question, perhaps, of finding the courage to say to him 'Come and see'.

A sense of purpose

When I was very young, about ten years old, there was a nun in our school who was quite different from all the others. Nowadays she wouldn't stand out so much, perhaps, because nuns do not go about in long habits, with their arms folded and hidden in great big sleeves, and with their eyes always cast down. But in those days such a sight was common, except, in our school, for this special nun who was at her best on the hockey pitch, racing up and down shouting instructions in all directions, and quite obviously living to the full. Even in the classroom she inspired one, with her energy, her directness and her complete common sense. We all loved her, as did our parents, because she was without guile. When she died, much too young, she was greatly missed, and school was never quite the same again.

Within the past few years I have been to see the sculpture of 'The Walking Madonna' by Elizabeth Frink, outside Salisbury Cathedral. This depicts Mary not so much walking as striding out purposefully, with long, determined steps, and, most interestingly, she is walking away from the Cathedral. It is as if, having been in there, she is going forward now because there is work to be done. There is joy, hope, purpose in the way she is depicted, and it struck me that anyone who might meet such a woman could not but be refreshed and invigorated by the meeting.

Perhaps the sculptor has got it exactly right ...

Delight: An experience of God

In his lovely book, *Towards a Civilisation of Love,* Basil, Cardinal Hume has the following very striking sentence: '(in anything undertaken) there should be a thirst for excellence ... and a sheer delight in the activity for its own sake'.

I find it a lovely thought. To experience such delight seems to me to be the essence of what it is to live a full life. We can often fail to notice the 'laughing' side of the Holy Spirit, and I suppose that this is understandable, since at present we see 'through a veil, darkly'. But obviously we are not seeing the whole picture, and we know this because every now and then something will lift even the most prosaic of us out of ourselves – a piece of music, perhaps, or of poetry; a person, perhaps, or a moment of love, can cause to flash across our consciousness a sudden experience of spontaneous joy and delight, and I feel that such an experience is a glimpse of things to come. After all, nothing that is created can be greater than its creator. Therefore I believe it follows that the source from whence these moments of delight come must surely be Delight itself.

In his book, *God of Surprises,* Gerard W. Hughes puts it another way: he says 'There is also laughter, merriment, and a lightness of touch when God is present'.

I find it a useful thing to remember.

Community

I heard Jean Vanier say once that community is a place where there will be pain. And he wasn't just speaking of institutional communities, but also of families. The fact is that pain is unavoidable when people live together, even when everyone works hard to live in communion.

I think it's part of the imperfection of humanity. Everyone is different, and people can have different perceptions, even of authenticity. For example, some people feel the need to be communicative, whereas others feel no such need. And if someone feels no need to communicate with me, then there is no use my feeling upset, just because I myself may be a communicative person. Should anyone force him or herself to communicate with me just to please me, that might be a very false gesture on that person's part, and therefore worth nothing.

If, therefore, I feel pain over this, I really must deal with it in myself, and not try to put it on to the other. The fact is that no-one has to conform to my expectations of him or her; contrary to the title of Paul Durcan's poem, I am not, after all, the centre of the universe!

This is a hard lesson to grasp, I think, and a salutary one, and it may well be one with which I may struggle through the whole of my life. But there is, it seems, no other way to the truth.

The fierceness of love

I know a small black dog whose enthusiasm for people is such that she greets them effusively by jumping all over them. Recently I heard someone telling her to desist, but almost immediately someone else came to her defence, by saying to the objector 'Do you not understand? It's just that she loves in a fierce way'.

I find that a marvellous expression. And indeed it epitomises for me many great loves. It seems to have been the way Peter loved Christ, judging by the way he jumped to his defence when the soldiers came to arrest him. Paul hated the Church fiercely, and then loved it equally fiercely when he changed sides. Christ himself was pretty fierce when he threw everyone out of the temple for love of his heavenly Father. And I have no doubt at all but that the woman who dried Jesus' feet with her hair knew the same kind of love for him. Such gestures demonstrate for me love at its simplest and at its greatest.

I think it is still around. You can see it in a teenaged son or daughter, fiercely defending his or her friend; in a mother or father defending an offspring; we know it in ourselves when someone lets us down and we make excuses for that person – an echo, surely, of the profound love in the saying 'They know not what they do'.

It seems to me to be no bad thing to love or be loved 'in a fierce way'.

Acceptance – of self

It isn't easy to let go of something, especially if it has been of great value to us. Even with the knowledge that to let go would be a good thing, it can still cause great pain. Sometimes one can make a decision to cut something out of one's life which can no longer be held on to, and even think for months at a time that one has succeeded. Then quite suddenly one can be thrown back again into the same difficulty and dependency as before.

And this can be disconcerting, especially if you have been feeling somewhat successful in your endeavours, and have been patting yourself on the back, even if cautiously.

This, I suppose, is where both patience and acceptance come in. This is where it becomes necessary to face the fact that there really is a problem, the problem, not so much of having a difficulty, but of recognising it and owning it as part of yourself, part of your very make-up.

What the learned ones say is this: accept the fact, and then you can begin to deal with it.

I suppose it is pride that prevents us accepting ourselves as we really are. And that is a pity. If, after all, we are acceptable to the one who created us, if we are accepted and loved by our very source, then who are we, with our little egos, to refuse to be accepting of ourselves?

None of this is easy to deal with, but it seems to me it is well worth tackling, and indeed it may be necessary to get help from others wiser than we are in learning to accept ourselves as we truly are. To do so may well turn out to be the first step in a journey towards living with reality.

There is one other point I would make in this regard: your head may well see the wisdom in this one day, but your heart may take a little longer. Just remember to give it time!

Gerald Manley Hopkins put it this way: 'My own heart let me more have pity on.'

Learning to wait

I once heard someone describing the living of life at its best as being 'the art of knowing when to let be, and when to be creative'. I found it a wonderful definition. I also thought that it is probably just about the hardest lesson we have to learn.

I think it is difficult to discern when to be quiet and when to take steps. And it takes time to learn this particular art, perhaps especially so if we are inclined to be somewhat impulsive. Sometimes I think there is a need to play for time, in order to get the balance right.

We have many examples in the gospels of people who took time to be reflective. We are told, for instance, that Mary took a little time before replying to the angel; and, further on, we are told that she 'pondered in her heart'. Jesus lived in a reflective way. We know this, because we are often told that he went apart. Sometimes his friends were annoyed with him for his tardiness, as, for instance, was Martha when he took so long to come when her brother, Lazarus, died: 'Lord, if you had been here, my brother would not have died'. Jesus, however, apparently needed time before calling to the house, maybe because he himself needed to come to terms at a personal level with the loss of a loved friend.

And so I find that I am left with a choice, very often: I can restlessly wear myself out with anxieties, or I can sink back into the business of waiting, and take on that actual waiting as part of the life which at this moment I am being asked to lead. Then the waiting must surely be a prayer in itself.

PART II

The experiencing and the telling

'... two of them were on their way to a village called Emmaus, seven miles from Jerusalem, and they were talking together about all that had happened. Now as they talked this over, Jesus himself came up and walked by their side; but something prevented them from recognising him ...

... he went in to stay with them. Now while he was with them at table, he took the bread and said the blessing; then he broke it and handed it to them. And their eyes were opened and they recognised him ... Then they told their story of what had happened on the road and how they had recognised him at the breaking of the bread.

Luke, 24

Journaling

Someone wrote 'Never write in your diary what happened on that day; you don't know what happened on that day'.

True enough! Of course there is the exception, the occasional time when someone will, for instance, be able to say with certainty that they fell in love at first meeting. But on the whole I believe it's fair to say that we cannot know how one small incident in the course of our day will set off a train of events – for good or ill – which may well stay with us for the rest of our lives.

In spite of this, however, I believe there is some value in sometimes keeping a journal of a kind. I find it especially useful if I cannot get myself down to praying in a formal or conventional way. Then, I find it useful to pick up my pen and write to God, as formally or as informally as I feel is necessary. Sometimes I may merely list for God the chain of disasters which has littered my day. And the very doing of this can somehow bring a sense of acknowledgement of the disasters; and that, in turn, may give me the opportunity to distance myself even the smallest bit from them.

It may not seem much of a prayer, but it may be my most authentic, and for that reason if for no other, I believe the one who is compassion will find it acceptable.

Language

'Above all,' the lecturer said, 'we are beings of language, and language is central to our humanness'.

I, of course, was delighted. It vindicated for me all the stumbling efforts at expression through words; the changings, the crossings-out, the trying again.

It's so easy to get it wrong! We try to make ourselves understood, but we get stuck because the right words escape us, or maybe we think they don't even exist. And I suppose that's why some people go to the trouble of learning a particular language, if they want to read a novel originally written in that language. I think it is often seen in a child's speech, because the child will not as yet have learned the convolutions of adult language.

Poets are sometimes wonderfully clear also – and sometimes I find they take my breath away by their accuracy. Micheal O'Siadhail is one such for me. Here are a few lines from his poem, *Autumn Report*, in which he writes about middle age:

> Even in this fall, wholehearted life reverberates
> Some almighty gaiety, invites me to adore
> The immense integrity; wines my veins until
> I'm sure my frame will warp under such
> Exuberance. I have never felt so near the centre
> Of all that is.

If we are lucky, we will at least occasionally have felt this same exuberance, I believe, and it is the recognition of this which can give us reason to hope. At least, that's how I hear those lovely lines.

Learning to live

In his beautiful book, *The Truth in Love*, Vincent Mac Namara writes that as a child he used to wonder why people didn't tell him everything, and then, as he thought, he could just get on with life from that point.

Of course, he discovered that the fact is that to know about life, one needs to live it. All the telling in the world won't do, it actually has to be lived through.

Thus did Mary and her Son go through thirty years of life together, learning in their daily living just what it is to live. And we are told that she 'pondered'. I am sure he did also, because, being fully human, he had to grow into knowledge day by day, often, no doubt, with as much pain as any other human.

When he left home, at approximately thirty years of age, it cannot have been very clear to his mother just why he went. Nor can she have fully understood the manner in which he set about things; and when stories and messages came back to her, reports of the odd situations he was at times found in, she certainly had much to ponder.

I sometimes think that it is an extraordinarily vulnerable state to be asked to live in, the state of pondering. And yet it seems to me also that at certain times in our lives it is the only course open to us. I think this certainly applies to parenthood, but perhaps it applies to many other relationships also.

And most difficult of all, perhaps, may be the thought that such pondering may never cease as long as we are in this life, since the final meaning of things is not within our reach while we are here. This, therefore, is probably where trust comes in.

It may also be, I think, that since the essence of prayer is truth, then the very state of pondering may well be authentic prayer.

Two miracles

One Autumn day, I witnessed two miracles. I was walking along a road on the outskirts of Dublin – an old road, with chestnut trees growing along each side.

I have been of the opinion that, living as we do in an impatient age, all chestnut trees which were in reach of many passing people were generally stripped of their fruits long before that fruit was ready to drop. I was therefore both surprised and delighted when I suddenly saw on the ground in front of me a large, shiny 'conker'. Its green shell, the inside still white, lay beside it. I darted forward and picked it up with great glee. And then, before I could straighten my back, I saw another, and another, and I moved forward and collected them all.

After a while I became embarrassed. I looked cautiously up and down the road, and was glad it was almost deserted – that is, except for the figure of a woman some distance away from me. Just as I became aware of her I saw her bend down suddenly, run a few steps, and then bend down again, gathering something up as she did so. We were getting closer each moment, and eventually, when we were within earshot, she held out her hand, full of chestnuts, and said to me 'I can't resist them', and she was smiling broadly. 'Neither can I,' I replied and then I added 'And may we never!'

Later, travelling in a bus, I took one of the chestnuts out of my pocket and examined it. Its colour and texture delighted me. And I fell to pondering this marvellous miracle, how that one tree could produce, year after year, such perfect fruit, having done so since long before my birth, and would probably continue to do so long after I was gone.

That was the first miracle; the second was this: that the first miracle, on that perfectly ordinary day, had caused two perfectly ordinary autumn women to quite literally jump for joy, proving yet again, I think, that the Spirit, the very essence which is each one of us, does not suffer the ageing process, and is not subject to mortality.

Newgrange

One mid-winter's day, just a few years ago, I was in Newgrange. There are a myriad wonderful facets to that experience, but one which held me in thrall was the experience of being caught in an extraordinary, vast rhythm. Here was a small group of people keeping vigil, standing on ground on which had stood other such groups as far back as 5,000 years ago. We waited, as they waited, for the first ray of sun to penetrate the chamber through the opening in the stonework; each group, 5,000 years apart, awaiting a sign of hope.

The awareness of this vast rhythm that day led me to become aware of other rhythms: the ebb and flow of the tides, twice a day, every day, year in, year out, decade after decade, millennium after millennium. And in the silence of Newgrange I also became conscious of the rhythm that was in each of us, as we breathed in and out; the rhythm of our very moods, even; of how we were now experiencing elation and joy, and yet it would inevitably follow that all too soon everyday life would catch up on us again, plunging some into pain, perhaps, others perhaps into anger, still others perhaps into fear.

But, so it is; nothing stands still. Vast or small, everything moves. There is, as I once heard someone say, only one absolute.

I am captivated too by the three-spiral symbol found carved out on one of the stones in Newgrange. I find it symbolic of the entire mystery of everything. It can represent so much; for one person, perhaps, the environment – that is, everything outside of that person; and the person her or himself; and thirdly, the creator. And looked at in this way, it becomes the eternal triangle, encompassing everything. Each of us becomes part of everything else; everything else becomes part of each of us; and all become part of the creator, without whom we would not be, at all.

The beginnings of such a belief awakens in us, I think, a knowledge that to damage anything or anyone is to damage ourselves; to diminish or destroy anything or anyone is to diminish or destroy ourselves, and is not only something which is against another but, ultimately, against ourselves and against *the* other.

In St John's gospel, Jesus prayed that we all might be one. The Newgrange symbol helps me to envisage just such communion.

Life's pace

It must be about ten years ago, or even more. We had five whole days to ourselves in Connemara, which was rare for us in those days of rearing a family. It was mid May, but the sun was so hot that you couldn't have expected better in July, and the greens and blues of the mountains were as they always are in the brochures. We had walked a long way into the mountains from the road, and when we came to a small stream it was inevitable that we would sit down and trail our feet in the water. We didn't talk much, and the only sound, apart from the stream, came from a lark so high in the sky that it seemed almost too much like work to try to seek him out.

We didn't notice the small boy until he was right beside us. His hair was red, like in all the postcards, and he was about four years old. The satchel on his back was about twice the size of himself. He sat down quite near to us, opened the enormous bag, took out a bar of chocolate, and began to munch.

'Hello' I said. He nodded. I thought I'd try again. 'What's your name?' He fixed me with an eye. 'Liam' he said, and I knew by the way he said it that my quota of questions was used up. None the less, some twenty minutes or so later, anxious motherhood overcame me, and 'Should you not be getting home, Liam?', I ventured, somewhat timidly. 'I'll wait for the cow', said

Liam. 'What?', I asked, not sure I had heard right. 'I'll wait for the cow' he said again, and pointed in front of us.

I shielded my eyes from the sun, and sure enough, after some moments I could dimly make out the shape of an animal coming down the mountain a long way away.

Half an hour must have passed, and at last the big brown cow loomed up beside us. Ignoring myself and my companion, she ambled straight over to Liam, bent her great head down, and gave him a nudge. All of a sudden he roared with laughter, punched her lightly on the nose, and, with the help of her head he scrambled to his feet, swinging his bag on to his back as he did so. He grinned widely at us, and he was totally transformed.

'Bye' he said. 'Bye' we said, and we watched him as he trotted after his large and lovely friend.

There is a certain shade of red hair, and when I am standing sometimes on a busy street, praying for the traffic lights to change so that I may be in time for work, I glimpse a red head that will put me in mind of Liam and of his amiable companion. And when this happens, I am grateful for the knowledge that somewhere, not very far from the daily noise of the city, life is lived at a gentler, and I would say a saner pace.

Saints with a small 's'

When I was at school, we were taught in Christian Doctrine class about the communion of saints – saints with a small 's', that is, the interlinking that exists between all humanity, those gone before us, those presently living throughout the whole world, and those still to come, interlinked in the mystical body of Christ. This belief seldom gives me difficulty. This is how I see it working:

When I was about ten years of age and on holidays at the seaside, I walked the length of the beach one day with a small visitor from England, also aged about ten. For almost the whole of the walk, he told me about his electric train set, and I was completely fascinated, because nobody I knew was the possessor of such a wonderful thing.

His name was Paul, and if I knew his second name then, I have long since forgotten it. I have no idea today whether he is alive or dead. None the less, whenever I set out to walk along a beach now, Paul comes into my mind. And I try to turn that flash of remembrance into an unspoken prayer for him and for all whose lives touch his.

As to how much value this has, who can be sure? But somehow to me it suggests that none of us is ever completely alone. Somehow, through this huge network of flashing thoughts, sudden remembrances, crossings of paths, crossings, even, of minds, each one of us is somehow connected to the other, and therefore to Christ, and therefore to the source of all.

It follows therefore, I believe, that it is within the capacity of all of us to help all others throughout the pilgrimage.

The human Jesus

Seville is a beautiful city, and stylish too, with its lovely riverside setting and the beautifully laid-out tree-filled parks all through it. Very near the Cathedral is the Latin quarter, and here the streets and squares are narrow and cobbled and beautifully kept. Every balcony is festooned with flowers, and in this colourful district it is possible to find a small hotel, or residence, offering a clean bed and breakfast for very little.

One evening as we walked a couple of hundred yards from just such a hotel in search of something to eat, we were attracted by a small restaurant, both by its fresh gingham tablecloths and the reasonable prices displayed on its menu.

Inside, the place was full of photos of bullrings and bullfights and matadors. We had in fact stumbled on a restaurant owned by a local hero, and the whole interior was crowded and noisy, where we seemed to be the only tourists.

They could not have been more welcoming. They were also extremely simple and straightforward, as was the meal which was served to us without fuss. We were given, with no trimmings, a basket of bread, a jug of wine and a platter of fried fish. And it was delicious.

And as we ate, it suddenly flashed into my mind that this was probably as near as I had ever come, as near, maybe, as I ever would come, to eating a meal which must have very closely resembled the meals which Jesus shared with his companions. And this thought affected me in two ways: firstly, I was struck by an extraordinary sense of continuity, that after all these centuries we were in many ways not living very much differently from the people of those long-ago times, and this in turn gave me a sense of belonging, of belonging to that same human race to which he belonged; and secondly and no less importantly, I had a sense at that moment of seeing him not as someone remote and inaccessible, but as very real; someone who had lived a real life, had eaten, drunk, laughed with and enjoyed the table fellowship of his friends – without doubt women as well as men – and in that moment I felt a sense of understanding him as really human, someone with whom all of us might with ease relate.

Generation gap

It has always looked to me as if it was a tricky start to a marriage; an out-of-wedlock pregnancy; nowhere for the child to be born; and later, having to travel many miles before finding a safe place in which to set up home. Joseph and Mary must have been highly delighted when they eventually got the opportunity to put down some roots in Nazareth, sort out their meagre possessions and set up his workshop. This seems to have been their first chance at getting some semblance of normality into their lives.

It seems reasonable to me that the relationships in that particular household must have been warm, and they must also have been together a lot, given that Joseph worked from home. What can it have been like, then, when for three days they lost their child? If you have ever lost a child in a supermarket even for a few moments, you will know the terror. And in the case of their loss, there were no telephones, no P.A. systems, no way of finding someone except by slogging on foot or horseback to cover all possible venues in person. I suppose that they split, Joseph going in one direction, Mary in the other, and when they met again, both having drawn a blank, their agony must have compounded, as the hours turned into days.

And it is my belief that when they eventually found him their feelings must have been mixed; relief, certainly, at finding him well and alive; astonishment at finding him preaching and being listened to by his elders; but maybe above all they felt a great deal of perplexity, not only that he should have gone away from them without explanation but also that when his explanation did come, it was so enigmatic.

And here, it seems to me, Joseph and Mary were confronted by a situation with which perhaps all parents are confronted, a situation where their offspring took a decision which they as parents simply did not understand. And no doubt it was not the only time, but one of many, when they both had good reason to 'ponder in their hearts'.

Encouragement

If you offer to help someone and the offer is refused, it's hard sometimes not to feel a bit peeved. If you hold out your hand to someone and that person turns away, you could be excused for feeling a bit sore. And of course it works the other way also; if you refuse a helping hand you may well imagine that person losing interest, and going away feeling disgruntled, feeling, perhaps, that they have done their bit, and giving up on you.

Not so with Jesus and the rich young man. Here was a fellow with a very good heart, and he obviously felt that he might perhaps do something more with his life than just have a good time. And so he stuck his neck out.

And in fact Jesus gave him a chance to get off the hook, as it were, but the young man pressed his point until in the end Jesus gave in and said something like 'All right, if you really mean what you say, come with me'. He called his bluff. And that, as we know, was more than they young man could manage. Brought to the point, he could not renounce his enjoyable life, and he 'turned away, sad'. In view of the fact that he had pressed Jesus, it would have been understandable if Jesus had displayed a certain impatience with him.

But of course we know that this did not happen; quite

the opposite. What happened was that in the very teeth of the young man's turning away, Jesus 'looked on him and loved him'.

What an extraordinarily compassionate response! And for all of us, who from time to time may feel a certain sense of failure to respond to another, what a consoling story!

More encouragement

When things are not going well for me, I tend to turn to Peter. He really was, from the gospel stories, a past master at putting his two feet in it.

Take his denial. In all the editions of the gospel that I have seen, Peter's denial of Christ is even written in heavy print. Sometimes I think we are glad to know of his discomfort, it gives us all excuses. No-one was holding a gun to Peter's head, nor twisting his arm; all that happened was that a persistent little girl kept coming up to him and asking him the same question. And Peter betrayed his friend. My heart goes out to him every time I read that story.

And then he worried about Christ's love for John, asking 'Where will he be?' He was full of peevishness, frailty, and probably just plain jealousy. None of this is too difficult to identify with, I find.

Even when he fought for Christ and maimed the soldier, Christ took the soldier's side. So, no matter what Peter did, it seems he simply couldn't get it right.

And yet, for all that, we know how special Peter was to Jesus. He left him in charge, and surely that was no small thing.

Yet more telling, I think, was the story of the two disciples on the road to Emmaus who rushed to the others to tell them and were greeted with 'We know, it is true; he has risen, and has appeared to Peter.'

In spite of his betrayal, then, Jesus wanted his friend to be one of the first to know the good news.

There's hope for us all!

Jesus, one of the laity

I often think that Vatican II came about because Pope John XXIII wanted to bring to the attention of all the members of the Church that at its foundation most of the members of the Church were lay. The numbers of ordained people, once ordaining had been arrived at, and the numbers of members of religious orders, has always been tiny in comparison to the number of lay members.

Jesus himself was lay of course, and his friends also. They lived ordinary lives, in the marketplace. In fact, Jesus himself points out that it was his cousin John who lived a life of austerity and fasting, but by all accounts, from the number of times it is mentioned, Jesus quite simply loved a party. He seems to have gone to celebrations of every kind, weddings, feasts; if there was a party on, he seemed to be in the middle of it.

And we also know that he set great store by table fellowship, in the long run using the symbols of bread and wine – for those around him at the time, the food and drink of the everyday – to institute his greatest gift of all to us.

I take great comfort too from learning that his table companions were as often as not a motley crew. He sat down to eat and drink with Pharisees and sinners, Jews, gentiles, tax collectors, the rich, the poor – and women! There was nothing elitist about any of the gatherings we are told about; no-one was black-beaned, no-one left out because she or he dug with the wrong foot, no-one left out because she happened to belong to the other sex.

And it therefore seems that Jesus, in the fullness of his humanity, lived out his life not in any rarefied atmosphere of prayer and silence, except on some specific occasions, but, by and large, as we all do, in the bits and pieces of the everyday.

PART III

Glimmers of understanding

To say 'Yes' to life, to receive it as a gift, is to accept everything as an interconnected unity. If that 'everything' includes murderous rejection, then that too is to be embraced by love.

Brendan Lovett: It's not over yet...'
(Claretian Publications, Quezon City, Philippines)

Unexpected prayer

In her book, *The Listening God*, Miriam Pollard gives the following definition of prayer: 'Prayer is a determining to accept our situation'.

Of all forms of prayer, communal as in liturgies, private prayers of petition perhaps, or thanksgiving, or contrition, that of determining to accept our situation seems to me to be the kernel. In it I hear the prayer of Jesus in Gethsemane, when, even though every fibre of his being abhorred what was coming to him, he was prepared to go ahead – and, further, he was also accepting of his own human, frail, completely understandable abhorrence.

On one occasion recently I found myself experiencing great fear. I tried to think of a formal prayer, but was unable to do so. The only words which were running round my head were 'I have never been so afraid in my life before'.

Later, I realised that this admission, because it was the absolute truth for me at that moment, was in fact the only prayer I could possibly have prayed.

Gift

In an article called 'The Spirituality of Waiting', Henri Nouwen suggests that the difficulty we all have with waiting is that it is not within our control. And I am sure he is right. There is something very difficult indeed about not being able to organise things, about taking a passive role, and letting things happen to us.

And we cannot speed up the process either. It is beyond our capacity. We might wish with all our hearts to be in a different frame of mind about something and yet be unable to achieve this. The most we can contribute may be to try to be open, so that if the opportunity for change (conversion) comes, we will be ready.

There are in fact a great many things I would like to feel different about in my life, but I don't feel different about. I don't like feeling annoyed, for instance, if I am left out of something of which I would very much like to be a part; I would be happier if I did not get upset when someone is sharp with me; I really dislike expending energy – energy which no doubt I could well make better use of – in wanting something which is not for me. I am sometimes upset when I am unable to respond to someone who might look for my help. And yet these things do happen.

Difficult feelings are not something which can be shed like an overcoat. They are far more tenacious than that.

They are, in fact, part of the human, very often imperfect, condition and the best that I can do with them is to suffer them, and wait until such time as I am handed the gift of their passing from me – if such happens.

Learning to wait is perhaps our most important task. To be aware that we have difficulty with this is, according to the learned ones, more than half the battle.

Friendship:
Reciprocity and Forgiveness

If proof were needed by me that Jesus was fully human and therefore capable of experiencing human emotions, then that proof is surely found in the story where he took with him Peter, James and John and went into the Garden of Gethsemane to pray. He was in crisis, and he needed the support of his friends at that particular moment. I find I can identify with that.

And if proof were needed by me that his friends were ordinary, then that proof is surely there also. Most of us, I suspect, will have experienced at some time in our lives the pain of having a friend come to us and say 'Where were you when I needed you?'

We probably know also of occasions when we went in crisis to find a friend, and found her sleeping.

It seems to me, therefore, that friendship is a matter of constant forgiving and of being forgiven.

And from the sheer, rueful humanness of this I take hope, because if we have experienced the beauty of friendship even at this human and imperfect level, does not the fact that we recognise it to be imperfect mean that deep down within us we are aware that we are all capable of so much more? And is not that knowledge, that sense of the 'not yet', an intimation to us of what we can hope to experience in eternity?

It is in such manifestations of human if less than perfect love that I place my trust.

Homage

There is, I find, great joy in watching an expert operating in his or her field, no matter what that field is, and I find this particularly so when the expert is a craftsman or woman. I invariably experience great elation, as well as wonder, when watching some apparently inanimate object turn into a thing of beauty before my eyes. Woodwork is one such craft, but above all I think the craft of the potter is one of the most fascinating. To see what at one moment appears to be a useless, shapeless lump of wet clay take form and become something of beauty and use causes me to wonder greatly. And I can understand why such pieces of clay and the story of their transforming are often likened by writers on spiritual matters to the life of a human being who, in the course of his or her journey through life is thrown and battered, shaped, honed and fired, in order to achieve her or his real potential.

Recently I was talking to a potter in Wicklow and was held in thrall by the skill of his hands as he worked. Among other things he was making beautiful goblets – vessels well suited, it struck me, to be used in a celebration of the eucharist.

As I picked up one of the finished cups, admiring its subtle texture, I discovered that near the base of the stem there was a band of clay which had not been glazed like the rest of the cup, but was still in its rough state. And then, looking at the other objects around me, jugs, plates, bowls, platters, I saw the same thing; on each, there seemed to be a line, or rim, which had not been given a glazed finish.

Puzzled, I asked the potter why this was so. And his answer I found both simple and profound. 'Homage to the clay', he said.

Wordless prayer, it seems to me...

'All shall be well'

I don't suppose anyone enjoys failure, and especially if one has put a lot of hard work into a thing. There's nothing very pleasant about watching that same work crumble to pieces. It seems to me to resemble the tide eating up a sandcastle.

And yet it happens all the time. We make great efforts, put a lot of hope into a project, and then along comes the sea, away beyond our control, sometimes with a roar but as often as not imperceptibly and yet just as insidiously, and in no time at all our beautiful castle is gone. And there is absolutely nothing we can do to save it.

Time is another problem. We spend lifetimes building something up and then watch its destruction in the blink of an eyelid. I always think of this when I see the felling of a tree; years of growth and nurturing and then, within minutes, total destruction with one efficient tool.

Is there an answer? Should we give up building? Should we give up planting trees? Hardly. Sometimes I think our very nature would make such a thing impossible. Humankind is such that most of us will go on hoping, against all the odds.

I once heard someone say 'If it fails, then let it be a noble failure'. I found this most helpful, because it seems to me to mean that even failure has a value, because at least it means that someone tried. And maybe it's the very trying, rather than the result, that counts.

Compassion

In many of the stories recorded about Jesus' life we hear about his wonderful compassion. In St Matthew's gospel we learn that on one occasion, when surrounded by a large crowd 'He felt sorry for them because they were harassed and dejected, like sheep without a shepherd'. In another we are told he said 'I feel sorry for these people because they have been with me three days with nothing to eat'.

And there are many other such stories; the healing of the woman who was haemorrhaging, for example, and the touching of the blind people so that their sight was restored.

And we ourselves are no different to those people whom he encountered. We are as much in need of compassion as they were. We make mistakes, we fail, we set ourselves tasks and then find we can't deliver. Facing our humanity and oftentimes our lack of success is not easy, and so it seems to me that we need to be able to extend compassion not only to others, but also to ourselves. Recognising our weaknesses and learning to take them on board as part of our unique personality, God given, needs to be seen as part of our compassion for humankind as a whole, and I think that it is sometimes to ourselves that we must turn with some degree of gentleness.

We would do well to remember this when we experience failure of one kind or another, I believe.

Out of order

There is something very poignant about the death of a young person, or, indeed, of anyone whose parents are still living. It doesn't seem to be 'in the right order', somehow. We all expect to be outlived by our children.

Perhaps because of the relationship Mary had with Jesus throughout the thirty years in which they lived together privately, and also perhaps because she was such an extraordinary person, with no doubt heightened depths of reflectiveness and understanding, she may somehow have prepared herself for his crucifixion. And with his, came her own, seeing that flesh of her flesh, whom she had nursed, washed, dressed, instructed, helped to grow and ministered to in every way, now torn and battered beyond recognition. She may well have recalled Simeon's words which she heard when her son was a baby, that a sword would one day pierce her heart.

And she could have been spared all of this, if she had died first. But for some reason or other, she was asked to stick it out, and carry that appalling cross.

I like to think that one of the reasons why this was asked of her was that it would give the rest of us courage when the going gets rough. I feel that it is helpful to know, somehow, that Mary knew it all at first hand herself. Knowing and recalling this fact makes it easier for me to remember to appeal to her for myself and others at critical parenting times.

On being human

Sometimes when I see someone with a very tidy desk, or kitchen, or garden, I envy them a bit. There is an attraction about orderliness. It seems to make life more simple. If, for example, you can put your hand out to pick up something where you actually left it down the day before and it is still there, there is a certain satisfaction in that.

Children dispense with this sort of order. Nothing stays in the one place. And this, it seems to me, more fully demonstrates life. On the whole, humanity is not always orderly, and we see all too often the most appalling examples of disorder on our television screens every day.

I believe it is worth taking a look at our own inner level now and then, to see how we are on order there, and oftentimes I think we may find that things are fairly chaotic. Take just one aspect of everyone's life, that of relationships. It is all too easy to chart a course as to how one might like a particular relationship to develop, but it doesn't work out like that at all. For some reason best known to her or himself, the other party may be looking at things in a different way, and she or he has every bit as much right to that point of view as I have to mine. And so, I may find myself in felt chaos.

And that, it seems to me, is how humanity is. That is how Christ was, often. None of his friends ever said that to be his friend was easy – in fact, quite the opposite. He demanded a lot from his friends at times and they often let him down. Peter is the prime example; Judas is another. I once heard that extraordinary man, Jean Vanier, say that when it is recorded on one occasion that the twelve 'went off to get food', Jean Vanier says that all twelve went, and not just two, or even four, because they couldn't take being around him any more!

But of course we also know that that is only one side of the story. And perhaps it's a side we should remember, when a relationship appears to be particularly difficult and untidy for ourselves. As was Jesus, we also are a part of humanity, and it seems certain that at times human relationship disorder may well be par for the course, for all of us.

Giving and Receiving

I know a chapel in Dublin where there is a tableau depicting Jesus washing Peter's feet. It's beautifully sculpted, and what strikes me most vividly about it is the utter confusion in Peter's attitude.

I don't agree with the saying that it is harder to give than to receive, at least, not all the time. For some, the business of giving seems so natural, so spontaneous, that is seems to be an extension of themselves. *Not* to give might oftentimes be much more difficult, at least for some.

But to be able to receive graciously is quite another thing. Supposing, for instance, one knows that what is being offered is of enormous importance to the giver – as was the case with the widow's mite; or supposing you feel embarrassed by another's generosity, what then?

When Jesus washed Peter's feet, Jesus had, to my mind, the easier part. Everything inside the other man was shouting out that he was not worthy of this expansive gesture on the part of his greatly loved and revered master. But Peter, once he heard Christ's reason for doing it, acquiesced, and I believe that he did this only with very great difficulty and at enormous cost to himself. And by so doing, he enabled Christ's message about the service of love to be proclaimed for all to hear, and to be told for all time.

I once read a beautiful description of the arts of giving and receiving; it said 'Both are graced endeavours'. And perhaps we could remind ourselves of this at times when we find ourselves lavishing something on someone with easy spontaneity. It may well be that the receiver has the more difficult part.

Hope

Peter, James and John were around at some of the most important moments, it seems, both the bad and the good. I suppose Mount Tabor balanced out Gethsemane in some way.

On Mount Tabor they were given a glimpse of the beauty of things to come. And so fantastic an experience was this that they did not, could not, speak of what they saw, that is, Jesus in all his glory, as God. It took some time before they were able to tell of seeing him 'in a new way'.

I remember someone saying to me once 'We will know each other in a new way' when we spoke of eternity. But, how are we to envisage this new way? How can we imagine anything which is not marked out and limited in time and space?

The fact is, of course, that we cannot, because our minds are finite. I once heard it said, however, that probably the nearest we will come in this life to understanding infinity is to compare it with a moment or moments in our lives when we have experienced pure love. And how can such a moment be described? The best that I can do is to say that for me such a moment seems to bring with it a sense of an all-embracing permeation of total peace, joy, wholeness, acceptance and of being finally and once and for all at rest.

In this I hope.

The difficulty of differences

I once read in a book on the scriptures the sentence 'A difficult man, this Jesus'. And so it seems he was, to many. We don't have to probe too deeply in the gospels to find this fact; witness the rich young man, who was totally unable to respond when asked to leave everything and follow him.

And he seemed to be equally difficult with his nearest and dearest. Over and over again he warned his disciples that following him would be no bed of roses. It seems he seldom gave them soft options. Recently I heard someone suggest that if all of this is true of him it may well have happened that one day, when he was thirty years old or thereabouts, he may have quite simply hung his tools up in the shed, walked across the kitchen floor to his mother, given her a peck on the cheek and said 'I'm off'. A difficult man indeed.

And we've all met such from time to time, and women too, for that matter. They can be hard to deal with, and maybe especially so if their ideas happen to be different from my own. But I suppose that they also, like Jesus, have their reasons, and sometimes it does seem to me that they are difficult because they have in them a passion for unrelenting truth.

And in this regard a somewhat awkward thought struck me recently: I wondered if it could possibly be that for them, our positions might be reversed? I suppose that could be so!

The price of love

Avila is a very small city, high up on the central plain of Spain. It has a fairy-tale quality about it because of its location and the wonderful golden coloured walls which surround it and which glow in the sunshine. Some of its streets, cobbled and crooked, are two thousand years old, and therefore it is not difficult to picture its most illustrious daughter, Teresa, walking through those streets over four hundred years ago.

She was by any standards a remarkable woman. As recently as 1970 the Roman Catholic Church proclaimed her a Doctor – the first time in its history that it bestowed such a title on a woman! She is also known as a great mystic, of which there have not been very many. And I also find it very interesting that she was well into middle age before she took on her great work of reforming the Carmelite houses throughout Spain.

But there are two much more mundane characteristics which endear her to me. The first is that a great part of her praying life seems to have been spent in arguing with her God, a familiar thing to many of us, I imagine. And the second is even more helpful: she seems to have had an enormous capacity to deeply love her fellow men and women – sometimes to the extent that it was difficult for her to keep those loves in perspective. She was a person who loved 'not wisely, but too well'.

I find it helpful to know that someone of Teresa's stature suffered such everyday pain.

Source of All

Some people are very moved by the beauty of music, while others may be tone deaf but may appreciate a beautiful land or seascape. Yet others will find all that is most beautiful in a single flower. Another may be most affected by poetry or prose. It varies greatly with different people.

There is a lovely book called *What is God?*, by John F Haught, and in it the author suggests that sometimes instead of thinking of God as a person, Father – or Mother – it can be very helpful to our prayer life to think of God as, for example, Beauty, or Truth, or Depth. I find this most helpful. I believe it means that if, for example, I find the depth of the colour of an African violet a most beautiful thing, or the astonishment in the eyes of a very young child, or the power of a particular phrase of music, as expressing beauty at its deepest, then I can think of God as the common denominator of all that extraordinary diversity of qualities, those qualities which lift me up and give me hope.

It is only in our finiteness and in the limitations of our language, that we are restricted to the small word, God.

PART IV

Journeying on

Beyond obedience, its attention fixed on the goal – freedom from fear.

And beyond that – love.

What next? Why ask? Next will come a demand about which you already know all you need to know: that its sole measure is your own strength.

Dag Hammarskjold: Markings

Adaptability

My friend had dropped in to see me, and I immediately offered to make coffee. But he said to me 'Never mind about the coffee, just sit down and listen to me'. And I was delighted to do so because it was only a sense of duty which had made me offer, and I felt that the listening was much more important at that moment.

When Jesus called on Mary and Martha, Martha was busy getting the dinner, and at first glance it might seem as if he rebuked her, which I find a bit rough. What was Martha to do, under the circumstances? There are many days when it might suit many people to curl up with a good book and stay away from the kitchen, but we know that we can't always do that. So what can we do then? I am slowly coming to the conclusion that there may in fact be no real solution to this particular problem; that in our imperfect world many of us may have no alternative but to muddle along, Mary one minute, Martha the next, and trust that we will continue to have the energy to make the transition as the occasion demands.

I have looked for a positive side to this everyday dilemma, and the one I have come up with for myself is this: that perhaps this small but persistent irritation is somehow symbolic, in that maybe it demonstrates to us a little of how our present world has imperfections, and maybe from this we can deduce that in the fullness of time, when we will come to know God and one another in total love and understanding, then the necessity to make these small and difficult choices will no longer be there.

There may be no need, then, to go and make the coffee.

Surprising sources of nourishment

I was slow in coming to appreciate the unique beauty of the Burren landscape. In fact, when I was young I found that barren-looking rock depressing, and failed to see its loveliness.

Recently, however, I experienced it in quite a different way, and I think this may have been because I somehow seemed to look at it in a different way. While before, I had only been aware of some of the tiny Alpine flowers that managed to grow in such apparently infertile ground, now I also saw the tiny trees, like Bonsai's, which grow completely flat, spreading out over the rocks in order to escape the harsh winds. And I realised for the first time that the plants were not so much growing *in spite of* the rock, but, more importantly, perhaps, they were thriving *precisely because of* the rocks which at first had seemed so hostile. And, looking at them in this way, I began to feel sure that those very flowers and trees are nourished by an essence contained in the rock, and that it is probably directly from this essence that they get their beauty and their strength.

I then began to muse on transposing this idea on to the growth of the human person. Life can often seem bleak and harsh for many, and there are times when there seems to be little comfort to be had from the immediate environment.

However, maybe we should look more closely. Maybe the very harshness with which we feel at odds is actually giving us the strength we need to live out our own potential and become what we may be. Perhaps to imagine such a thing will help us to feel less threatened by difficulties in our lives, seeing them as a source of nourishment, and this in turn may help us to live with our difficulties in some sort of harmony.

Balance

More often than not, it seems to me, when people speak of tension in their lives they speak of it as something which everyone would be better off without, but I feel that that is not the full picture. Certain tensions are necessary, I believe, in the daily living out of our lives and the lives of most created things. And a striking example of this can be seen in the very ordinary, and extraordinary, cobweb. By any standards its balance is remarkable, each strand being held in place by every other, giving the wonder of the whole. One thread breaks and the web is askew, and not quite so effective.

In such a way, I believe, are our lives balanced. Tension exists between all our different parts, each holding the other. And it is only when one strand snaps that we find ourselves in some difficulty.

It follows also, I think, that, just as the breaking of one thread in a web does not cause total collapse, neither need one difficulty of ours case us to disintegrate. With any luck, the other strands of which we are made up will keep us in some sort of shape, and we will continue to function, even if a little askew.

Likewise, I believe we can apply this analogy in a wider context, that of the whole human race. There may be times when we ourselves feel strong and in no obvious need of support from others; at other times, however, we may find ourselves less so, and not really in a position to carry on alone. Then I think we must become aware that there will be others who will at that moment be in a position to hold us until we are ready to bear our own full weight again. The world will not come to a standstill, and we will for a time be supported by stronger threads, to see us through a difficult time.

And it seems to me that this interweaving is exactly what Jesus was talking about when he prayed, as we read in St John's gospel, that we may be one. It is also, I feel sure, the true meaning of communion.

Searching for permanence

As I read a book one day on bereavement and loss, I read the following: 'It is one of the tragedies of life that very often those whom we love most are not with us when we most need them – and one of the glories that they sometimes are.'

I find this both profound and true. In my own experience, in order that I may fully appreciate a moment of beauty I generally wish that I might share that moment with another, and I imagine that I am not alone in this. Likewise, it seems to me to be easier to cope with the bad times if there is someone with whom to share them. And indeed, not to be able to do so often seems like a tragedy.

I also find that it is often the very absence of such a person that I am most aware of, whereas it would be a much happier thing if I could concentrate on the second point, and become more aware of the fact that sometimes those I love *are* beside me when I most need them. Such moments are surely bonuses. I also believe that they are glimpses of the 'not yet'.

And sometimes I ask myself why do these moments have to end? The answer seems to me to be in the title sometimes given to human lives, that we are pilgrims. Pilgrims by their very nature must move, because to be such one must be journeying. To endeavour to stand still is a nonsense. Therefore to try, sometimes, to remain in one place, to stay with him or her whom we love, is not always a real option. And the moving on can often make for great loneliness and longing. But this very longing in itself gives grounds for hope, it seems to me, because I believe it demonstrates our capacity for the more than transient; I believe it shows our capacity for an abiding state, abiding communion, abiding love.

And on this I base my hope.

Letting go

They tell us that practice makes perfect, and I'm sure there's a lot of truth in it but I don't for a moment think it's the whole story, not by a long shot.

Take the matter of letting go. Many, I believe, find it very difficult to let go, even in small matters. If we have to let go of an ambition, a project or an idea, that's even harder. And it is probably harder still for parents to let go of the next generation. Parents spend an enormous slice of their lives looking after their offspring, and then the day comes when, once they are strong enough to stand alone, that is exactly what the offspring do. As parents, we have seen this day coming for years. Indeed, we have encouraged it, and we even now know it is right. None the less, there is still, in most cases, great pain.

Perhaps with practice we can learn to let go perfectly. Maybe the majority of parents let go most perfectly. But it seems to me that perfection is one thing, and lack of pain is quite another. They may not be compatible.

And maybe that's the lesson we have to learn in the letting go, that, no matter how perfectly – or imperfectly – we do it, it is going to cost us dear. And it may well be that learning to live with the experience of that cost is what is important.

Towards the unknown

We are great for building walls around ourselves. We lock ourselves inside barriers, for safety's sake, because life can be tough, and we don't really want to walk into trouble.

We may, however, be passing up chances of experiencing new life, and that is a pity. Sometimes we do so by insisting on holding on to the familiar, because we feel safe with something we know, and to let go means to trust to the unknown. We sometimes lack this trust because of fear of pain, which no-one rushes into with much enthusiasm.

Staying wrapped up in cotton wool, however, is curtailing. We were probably never safer than when we were in our mother's womb, and yet that was not a full life as we now know it. Better, then, that we might venture a little .

This pondering on the things of which we do not yet know helps me whenever I'm subdued by the thought that perhaps after all there may be nothing beyond this life. I ponder on the fact that prior to birth I didn't know about this present life, and yet it was there. Why should the same not apply in relation to the next stage?

And then I push this a step further; it seems to me at times that the very fact that a thought of infinity is possible must surely make the possibility of such infinity possible. And in this I try to trust.

The great healer

Patrick Kavanagh said once 'Time has its own part to play'. And how right he was, especially, I think, in the matter of the pain of loss.

Time takes away the sharpness of the pain, little by little, day by day, month by month, so that the searing pain is less in complete charge from first waking moment till last. Bit by bit it becomes possible to experience other feelings and perhaps eventually even to be able to speak of the pain. The difficulty, of course, is the waiting. It can't be speeded up, and there is generally nothing to do but try to take it on board, and work through it as best I may.

This gives a sense, I think, of how little we are in control of things. It is, I find, a good example of the fact there is something, someone else, with ultimate control.

Such an acknowledgement may at times be frustrating, but at other times, and especially if we feel we may have made a mess of something, it is quite helpful to acknowledge that, as someone once said to me, 'It's all right anyway!'

The ultimate act of faith, maybe! And if we find we can only make it when the chips are down, does that really make it any less worthy? If compassion and love count for anything, then I doubt it!

Keeping in touch

I have heard criticism of the fact the sometimes we don't bother much about praying as long as things are going well for us. It seems that when we are on the crest of a wave there is no great urgency about keeping in touch with God, because we feel we can manage very nicely on our own. And then something goes out of kilter, and we come running. I have heard it said that this may be a poor thing.

I wonder; maybe the way God keeps in touch with us is by reminding us that we are not always at our best on our own.

At the end of Francis Thompson's beautiful poem, *The Hound of Heaven*, God is given the chance, as it were, to speak. The lines go as follows:

> All which I took from thee I did but take
> Not for thy harms,
> but just that thou might'st seek it in my arms.
> All which thy child's mistake
> fancies as lost, I have stored for thee at home;
> Rise, clasp my hand, and come.

A beautiful, poetic way of extending God's offer of help to us, as I read it.

The fact that some of us may wait until we are in trouble before seeking help cannot, I believe, make our prayer any the less acceptable. The very acknowledgement that we need help may well be the very way in which we find God – and in which God finds us.

The deafening silence

Sometimes I think God's silence is the hardest thing of all to accept. We try to pray as best we can – which may more often than not not be much – and we try to trust; we try to have faith, and to believe. And in return we are met with a wall of silence.

This can be disconcerting, but I think it is also a common experience. There are some, I know, who genuinely feel at times that their prayers are answered in very direct ways, but by and large I think this is not very often claimed.

There is a lovely little book by Karl Rahner, called *Encounters with Silence,* and in it the author writes of this very problem, the problem of trying to continue dialogue in the very teeth of apparently no response. And he points out that Christ himself experienced that very same silence when he most needed comfort, as he died on the cross.

I am glad when I remember this, because it gives me the opportunity of joining my pain of apparent abandonment to that of Jesus, and I take comfort from the knowledge that somehow or other in the abandoning silence I am, in fact, in good company.

Co-passion: sharing the pain

The word 'compassion' is, I think, a very lovely word, and is used to describe feelings of love and sympathy, and pity in the best sense, which are evoked in a person because of another's pain. To try to stand in the other's shoes, understand their pain and share in it so far as is humanly possible means co-passion, or compassion.

In the course of most lives there will with any luck have been times when compassion was extended to us by another. Perhaps some will also know that on occasion it has been possible for them to extend compassion to another. I believe that this human compassion is an extension of the compassion which is constantly extended to all of humanity by the one who *is* compassion. If I can give or receive compassion, and, perhaps most important of all, if I can sometimes remember to extend compassion to myself, then it seems to me that I am caught into that source from whence all compassion and love come.

And this, I believe, is where we may eventually hope to rest.

PART V

Towards Wholeness:
Women's perspective – the missing link

Until the world transcends the sin of sexism, the world can never be whole.

Joan Chittister, O.S.B.

Imaging God

To think of God in the feminine is nothing new. Yet today sometimes people blanch visibly at the suggestion. God, to be God, has to be beyond everything that we can name, including gender, and therefore when we use the term 'him' or 'her' to describe God it is merely a convenience of speech for ourselves, which comes about because of our inability to find any other way of describing the source of all.

Throughout the ages, people have on occasion spoken of God as feminine; Julian of Norwich and Hildegarde of Bingen did so, and I believe it occurs several times in the bible.

Within the past few years I came across an example in a poem painted on a sixteenth century crucifix which is hanging in St David's Cathedral in Wales. The poem is called *I am the Great Sun,* and here are the first two verses:

> I am the great sun, but you do not see me.
> I am your husband, but you turn away.
> I am the captive, but you do not free me,
> I am the captain you will not obey.
>
> I am the truth, but you will not believe me.
> I am the city where you will not stay,
> I am your wife, your child, but you leave me.
> I am that God to whom you will not pray.

Ministry

It does appear that, in today's Churches, to be a woman with a wish to participate actively in the ministry of Christ, it is necessary that she look for, find, and above all hold on to any encouraging signs that can be found. And I have discovered that this is best done by going back to the time of the founding of Christianity, to the Founder himself, and to look at the way in which he involved women in his ministry, crossing all barriers to do so. This is seen in the story of the woman at the well, when, having touched her heart, he sent her to 'Tell the others'. He did it again when he involved the woman who anointed him by telling those who protested that she had 'done what it is in her power to do; she has anointed me for my burial'. And there are other such examples, which must be sought out, and highlighted, it seems to me.

Are there really theological problems to the involving of women into full participation in ministry? Or are the problems brought about by tradition only? This not to say that tradition does not have a value, of course it has. But time brings change, and change is inevitable in anything that lives. A Church which cannot change is dead.

Many of us were brought up in a strict tradition, and it really does take a great leap of faith and imagination for such people to open up and say to women with regard to full ministry 'Yes, it's all right; come and join us'. It probably takes a prophet, and there are few enough of those around. Christ was *the* Prophet, and Pope John XXIII appears to have been one also. Slowly, their ideas are beginning to take root.

If you look up the word 'Feminist' in the dictionary, you will find it defined thus: 'A supporter of women's claims to be given rights equal to those of men'. This sounds a valid claim. And the word 'Christian' means one who follows Christ. Join these two words together, and it seems a most reasonable thing that a person would call her- or himself a Christian Feminist. And yet it poses a question for me, and it is this: It is possible to be a feminist without being a Christian; but is it possible to claim to be a Christian, without being a feminist?

Food for thought, surely!

The people of God

People define ministry in different ways. Some see it as a word relating only to the ordained; others broaden it to include those who through the structures of the various Churches spend their lives in recognisable actions through those Churches, in helping others; still others see it as part of everyone's everyday living.

I like the last definition best. It seems to me that all work lovingly undertaken to help one's fellow men and women can truthfully be considered ministry.

I once heard of a conversation between an ordained minister and a middle-aged married woman who expressed an interest in serving others through her Church. 'Do you know anything about ministry?' he asked her, and she replied ''I have been ministering for the past twenty-five years'. He took her point.

It can be disappointing for some when they are refused the outward signs of a particular ministry, and undoubtedly it would sometimes be handy to have a badge or a label as a distinguishing mark. But there can be occasions also when the very lack of such a mark may be a good thing, and an advantage. These days, when many have broken away from 'traditional' religion, one can sometimes be more acceptable by the very fact that one is 'ordinary'.

Not being free to work full time in recognisable, traditional ministry need not deflate lay people either. St Paul was a sail-maker by trade, and I presume, therefore, that he worked at a secular level for his bread and butter. It may be worth remembering these facts in the middle of a very ordinary day's work in the market-place, which is where the majority of us spend the greater part of our lives. We may well be ministering, none the less.

Everyday ministry

I have recently been very struck by the fact that, as I see it, ministry is reciprocal. There are examples of this all around us; a parent ministers to a child and the child, by its unconditional love, ministers to the parent in return; someone ministers to the sick, and is ministered to in return because of that person's acceptance of her or him who ministers. In everyday life, this reciprocity is to be seen everywhere.

So it was in the everyday life of Jesus. He ministered even to those who seemed to minister to him. He asked the woman at the well for a drink of water, as if he wished her to minister to him, whereas in fact this was his way of engaging her so that he could minister to her at a much deeper level. He washed the feet of his apostles so that they would learn from him how he felt he and they could best carry out his father's will. And no doubt during his private life when he was at home with his mother in Nazareth, they ministered to each other.

For most of us, the daily opportunities for ministry are probably myriad. We might, however, miss some of them, because of everyday noise and bustle. It does seem that some 'listening time' in the course of the day is essential. Certainly, Jesus found this to be the case; he frequently, we are told again and again, 'went apart'. And I often think that perhaps those times were times when his prayer may quite simply have taken the form of being still, and listening.

Vocation

We have always been taught that we are all members of the Body of Christ, and that includes men and women. To think of a body made up of many parts, we know from our own bodies that in order for all to be well, each part of that body needs to be well. If each part functions as it should, then all will be well overall.

It seems to me that in the body of the Churches, the potential of women members has not yet been fully released, and women do not as yet function to their full capacity. This means that the overall body cannot function to its full potential either.

Many worry about the recent marked falling off a traditional priestly vocations and vocations to the religious life. It seems to me that the meaning of vocation is changing, and that many women and men wish to play their full part in the working of the Body of Christ, but not in the traditional power structures which have for so long prevented half the members – women – from taking a full part. Therefore, as I see it, once the structures of the Churches can recognise and accommodate women fully, the Body of Christ will be able to fulfil itself in a much fuller and whole way.

It is for this recognition, I believe, that we must pray.

The reciprocity of ministry

There is something very real about the fact that Mary headed straight for Elizabeth her cousin and woman friend, when she found she was pregnant. I think she did this for two reasons: to help Elizabeth in her confinement, but also to share her own news with someone who would understand. Humankind doesn't change that much over the centuries, and these two women must have had a lot in common, a lot to talk about.

And so I see them as ministering to one another, and this, I believe, is what ministry is all about. We are, in fact, Christ to one another, because he has no-one else to minister for him. Bringing the eucharist to patients in a hospital, I thought at first that I had the ministering role. How quickly my mind was changed for me! How quickly it was brought home to me that the patients by their very acceptance of me, ministered to me, by a look or a word or a touch. And this reciprocity seems to me to be the real meaning of Church.

Mary and Elizabeth knew well how to minister. Most women know the same; it's in their nature, more often than not.

It is a pity if this fact is not recognised by those in charge in the Churches, because by not recognising it the Churches are wasting a precious resource.

Jesus' chosen friends

Jesus had women friends, we know that for a fact. There was his mother; there were Martha and Mary; there was Mary of Magdala, and, indeed, to her he chose to appear first, after his resurrection. There was the woman at the well, the woman who dried his feet with her hair, and the woman who had the audacity and courage, the wisdom and insight, the knowledge and love, to actually anoint him.

And what have these last three in common? The fact that they are nameless. Because they were women, it seems that no-one bothered to record their names.

I am curious, too, about the two disciples whom Jesus met on the road to Emmaus. One was called Clopas, a man's name, and recorded. The other person's name goes unrecorded. I wonder why? Was it because this other was in fact a woman? Remember, one of these two disciples reported that when they encountered Jesus and spoke to him their 'hearts burned inside'. Could that person have been a woman? I believe so.

Called to ministry: The woman at the well

In the various stories of Christ's personal encounters with others, more often than not there is a group involved; he is often with his friends, and engaged with more than one person. Often even when he goes to pray, he has brought company with him.

Not so, however, when he encounters the woman at the well – one of the people in the gospel whom I love most, because of her sheer humanity. Here, we have an uncommon chance of seeing Jesus in a one to one relationship. One thing is clear, and that is that this is no superficial relationship. For me, much of its attraction lies in the directness of the communication between the two. And yet, for all that they are both so direct, there is a level of gentleness and even tenderness which speaks volumes.

To begin with, Jesus, realising just how vulnerable this woman is, puts himself at the receiving end by asking her for a drink, thereby, I believe, giving her an opportunity to respond gently to him, and to respond with simplicity. And it does seem to me that, immediately realising that this man is not content with small talk, she responds with wonderful humility. It is undoubtedly true that there is great painfulness in acknowledging our wounds and our needs, but that is exactly what she did.

And, as I see it, because of this marvellous generosity Jesus then, with no ambiguity whatever, called this woman to direct ministry, when he told her to 'Go and tell the others'.

Isn't it extraordinary, then, that – it seems because of her gender – her name remains unknown, to this day.

Called to Ministry: She who anointed him

One day a lecturer said, when we were studying scripture, 'Take a piece of the text, and grapple with it'. I thought it was a great idea.

And so I grappled with the story of the woman who anointed Jesus. And one thing that struck me was just how much Jesus recognised the wholeness of women, both in human and in spiritual terms.

Then I studied it a bit more. And for the first time I took cognisance of the whole of the statement 'Leave her alone; she has done what it is in her power to do; she has anointed me for my burial.'

And so I began to grapple with that sentence. What did Jesus mean by it? Did he mean that it is in the power of everyone to anoint another? Or did he mean that this woman was a person who could be ordained a priest?

It is a very intriguing point, I think, and a very serious one. After all, if he stated clearly – and he evidently did – that it was in the power of that woman to anoint him for his burial, at what stage in the history of the Church was that power taken from women? And why? And by whom?

I believe that these are the sort of texts with which not just women, but all who purport to be Christians, must grapple.

Called to Ministry: Veronica – unafraid

The atrocities committed in every corner of the world which constantly appear before our eyes on television pose many problems. And often they are accompanied by an enormous feeling of helplessness. I remember reading an account by a woman writer of how some reporters stood immobile when someone was being killed in Northern Ireland, and she herself posed the question 'Why did none of us intervene?'

And there, I suppose, is the difficult side of humanity. How often does it happen in everyday life, even in small matters, that we are frozen into silence, even when we might wish with all our hearts to take action? The spirit can indeed be willing and ready, but the flesh doesn't always measure up, and the opportunity to take the side of the underdog passes us by, simply because at that particular moment we lack courage.

Sometimes I think our sins of omission include being unable to praise at the right moment, and maybe especially the young. It may come from some false sense of being afraid to spoil them. And in Ireland I think we find it very hard to extend a hand, or to say to someone 'I love you.' I wonder why it is so alien to us?

As depicted in the Stations of the Cross, Veronica was different. She took that step forward, to wipe his face –

the only comfort she could hope to give him at that moment. I often wonder was she a friend of his already or was this very simply the wonderfully compassionate gesture of an extraordinarily courageous woman towards a broken-down stranger. It doesn't matter which she was; she made the gesture, it seems to me, in total spontaneity, and one way or the other it was the very stuff of which love at its most profound is made.

Called to Ministry: Mary

I see Mary as a feminist. I see her son as one also. Of course there are times when I imagine he might have made life simpler for many of us if he had included one, just one, woman among the twelve. But he didn't – because of the times that were in it, I'm sure – and so, we have to work from there ...

By all accounts, Mary went her own way, as she thought fit. When, for instance, she pointed out to her son that their hosts at Cana were in difficulties, his answer was, to my mind, a bit sharp, maybe. But recently I read an interesting possible explanation for this in a book called *The Gift of Feeling* by Paul Tournier. He says that with much reflection he has formed the opinion that when Mary told Jesus that there was no wine, and looked to him to solve the problem, he answered sharply because he had not at that stage realised that it was now time for him to begin his public life. Dr Tournier holds that it was given to Mary to be the instrument through which Jesus learned that his visible life was to begin.

Thinking of Mary in this way, another thing struck me: when her son was a tiny baby, she brought him to the temple, and offered him up to God at the altar. Could this mean, I wonder, that she was in fact the first priest?

Ministry: unreasonable prohibitions

Everything St Paul said is not helpful to me as a woman, but one thing is very helpful. He said that we must 'Put on the mind of Christ'. I find this helpful if I have a dilemma on my hands. If I do not know what to do in a given situation, then the bottom line for me is to ask myself 'What would Christ have done in this particular circumstance?'

And we all know that he would not necessarily have done the conventional thing. Time and again we are reminded that he was not bound by hard and fast man-made rules. And least of all was he bound, it seems, when it came to the treatment of women. We know that he was fully mindful that they, too, are made in God's image and likeness. He included them in all sorts of situations, against the norm at the time.

And again, it is the woman who anointed him that springs to my mind. 'She has done what it is in her power to do; she has anointed me for my burial'. That was the mind of Christ.

Again I ask the question: Where is the mind of Christ in the prohibition?

Church: Women's understanding

There is much to give us hope and optimism just now, it seems to me. Since the ordination of women into the full priesthood in the Church of Ireland I feel a newness and freshness around, and a lifting of the nation's collective heart. At the first ordination of a woman, there was much joy, much crossing of barriers, as members from different denominations participated. It all seemed right and fitting.

As I attended that ceremony a thought crossed my mind, and it was this: when the other Churches can accept women fully, then Church unity will surely come about. It seems simple, and logical. Women, by and large, know what it is to give life, and they know the cost. Because of this I believe that they are not very interested in wars and divisions; such things are alien to their nature.

It should follow, therefore, as I see it, that if the hierarchies in the various Churches were balanced, with an equal number of women belonging to them as men, then the differences between Churches would begin to take on less importance. The women in the hierarchies would focus on the reconcilings, and the result would be a further movement towards the unity for which Jesus himself longed when he prayed 'That they all might be one'.

Love, justice, and women in the structured Churches

Most of us, most of the time, are locked into a system or systems, and even if we don't agree with that system and may wish to get out of it, it may be very difficult to do so. Many never succeed, for all sorts of reasons, and most of those reasons are probably legitimate. It can be very hard, for example, in fact it may be impossible, for someone who is economically dependent on a system to give up that dependence, since everyone needs to eat.

And that, to my mind, is part of the reason, and a very large part, why many women throughout the world, throughout our own country, and indeed, throughout the different Churches, find it such a struggle to fight for justice for themselves and for other women.

It is my firm belief that when Jesus said 'Blessed are the poor', he was referring to the majority of women in the world. I recognise that there are degrees of poverty, of course, and I know that we in this part of the world cannot compare our poverty with the starving peoples throughout the world. I realise that we must do all we can to persuade our own government and the other governments in wealthy countries to begin to take responsibility for justice throughout the whole world.

But here on our own doorstep we may be able to do

something more, by looking for justice both within society and within the churches. And this could begin to be done by looking for justice for women.

When Jesus lived his earthly life, women were locked into poverty and subservience; they had no weight, no education, no say, even in the matter of their own lives. And Jesus defied the system when he treated women as fully human and fully spiritual, putting them on a par with men.

It seems to me, then, that it must follow that those who are today engaged in what is known generally as Christian Feminism are the people who at this moment in history are most accurately carrying on his work, and I would push this even further and say that not to be a feminist, in this sense, is not to be fully a Christian.

Women in society at large, and in the Churches in particular, are the poor. And this is where, it seems to me, we must try to bring about change.

Sexism: The core injustice

Joan Chittister, the Benedictine theologian, believes that the women's movement is one of the great movements of all time, as was the Ice Age, Evolution, The Industrial Revolution. She sees the emergence of women as something that is here to stay, because she believes that once women come to believe in their own worth they will never sell themselves cheaply again. And when this happens, she believes, humanity will cease to be only half living. In fact, she says that because of patriarchy 'Humanity walks on one leg, sees with one eye, thinks with half its brain – and it shows'!

And so she suggests that we get in there, and bring about change. As far as possible this should be done without hurting anyone. She suggests that we become 'serpents who don't sting – but who keep on hissing'!

We must, she insists, keep thirsting for the fullness of life, and if we do this we will be spurred on and add our tiny bit to the new envisioning of roles, which will eventually help to bring about the wholeness for which all humanity longs. And she also adds sadly that it is probably necessary, even if painful, that women develop a 'theology for the long haul'.

To finish, I quote her again: 'Until the world transcends the sin of sexism, the world cannot be whole'.

There is much to be done, and we can all help, by the power of the Spirit, who blows where she will, regardless of gender. Let us heed her.